FOOTBALL'S RISING STARS
CAM NEWTON

Parker Holmes

PowerKiDS press™

New York

Published in 2013 by The Rosen Publishing Group, Inc.
29 East 21st Street, New York, NY 10010

First Edition

Editor: Matt Monteverde
Book Design: Dean Galiano

Photo Credits: Brian A. Westerholt/Getty Images, p. 5 Streeter Lecka/Getty Images. p. 7 Orlando Sentinel/MCT via Getty Images, p. 9 Bill Frakes/Sports Illustrated/Getty Images, p. 11 Kevin C. Cox/ Getty Images, p. 13   Kevin C. Cox/Getty Images, p. 15 Chris Trotman/Getty Images, p. 17 Jared C. Tilton/Getty Images, p. 19 Scott Cunningham/Getty Images, p. 21 Scott Cunningham/Getty Images, p. 22 9 Bill Frakes/Sports Illustrated/Getty Images, Chris Trotman/Getty Images, Back Cover Streeter Lecka/Getty Images

Library of Congress Cataloging-in-Publication Data

Holmes, Parker.
 Cam Newton / by Parker Holmes. – 1st ed.
    p. cm. – (Football's rising stars)
 Includes index.
 ISBN 978-1-4488-9190-0 (library binding) – ISBN 978-1-4488-9203-7 (pbk.) – ISBN 978-1-4488-9204-4 (6-pack)
 1. Newton, Cam 1989- 2. Football players–United States–Biography. 3. Quarterbacks (Football)–United States–Biography. I. Title.
 GV939.N42H65 2013
 796.332092–dc23
 [B]
                                                2012004432

Manufactured in the United States of America

CPSIA Compliance Information: Batch #WS13PK: For Further Information contact Rosen Publishing, New York, New York at 1-800-237-9932

CONTENTS

A RISING STAR

Cam Newton is one of the best new quarterbacks in football. He's awesome! Cam led Auburn University to a college national championship. He won the Heisman Trophy for being the best college player in the country. Then, in his first year in the National Football League (NFL), he set records as a Carolina Panther.

Cam has the **talent** of a superstar. He broke the record for most passing yards by a **rookie** NFL quarterback in 2011. He also set the record for most **rushing** touchdowns by any quarterback in NFL history. And you know what scares his **opponents** the most? He's so young that he's probably only going to get better.

Cam throws the ball during his first year with the Carolina Panthers. He had one of the best rookie seasons of all time.

HIGH SCHOOL HERO

Cam was born in Savannah, Georgia, on May 11, 1989. His full name is Cameron Jerrell Newton. But everyone calls him "Cam." Cam grew up wanting to be a football player like his dad. His family was very good at sports. His dad tried out for an NFL team. Cam's older brother, Cecil Jr., has been an offensive lineman for NFL teams.

Cam went to high school in Atlanta, Georgia. He played football and basketball there. He was a star quarterback. Cam was so good that many colleges wanted him to play for their team. He chose to play football for the University of Florida Gators, starting in 2007.

Cam passes the ball during a practice game at Florida. Cam started his college career at Florida, but he finished it at Auburn.

TIGER TIME

When Cam went to Florida, the team already had a good quarterback—Tim Tebow. Cam was a **back-up** quarterback for Tebow. During his second year, Cam hurt his ankle and didn't play the rest of the season. After two years at Florida, Cam moved to Blinn **Junior College** in Texas. Cam got to start as quarterback there. He helped Blinn win the national junior college championship!

Cam played so well that he wanted to **transfer** to a school with a big-time football team. So Cam moved to the state of Alabama and became an Auburn Tiger in 2010. Auburn University has had a lot of great football teams over the years.

Cam likes to smile and have fun. But he also likes to win. Auburn fans were really happy Cam decided to become a Tiger.

BIG AND TALL

Cam was a hero at Auburn. In his first game, he threw for three touchdowns and ran for two more. While at Auburn, Cam became the first player in the Southeastern Conference (SEC) to pass for 2,000 yards and run for 1,000 yards in a single season. Cam ended up with more rushing yards in a single season than any SEC quarterback in history.

Cam is really fast. Cam is also big for a quarterback. He's 6 foot 5 and 250 pounds. So he's tough to tackle. Most quarterbacks can throw a lot better than they can run. But Cam is really good at both passing and running. Cam has the arm of a quarterback, the legs of a running back, and the size of a linebacker.

Cam runs by a couple of Louisiana State players. Cam ran the ball for 217 yards and two touchdowns against LSU.

NATIONAL CHAMP

Auburn had an 11-0 record going into the 2010 game against the University of Alabama, their biggest rival. If Auburn lost, they might not go to the national championship game. Auburn quickly fell behind 24-0. It wasn't looking good for the Tigers. But guess who came to the rescue? Cam Newton! With time running out, Cam threw for three touchdowns and ran for one more. Auburn won 28-27.

Cam led his team to an undefeated regular season. Then he helped Auburn win a national championship against the Oregon Ducks. He was so good in 2010 that he won the Heisman Trophy. Cam had one of the greatest seasons in college football history!

Cam celebrates after winning the SEC Championship Game against the South Carolina Gamecocks. Auburn beat South Carolina 56-17.

13

TOP PICK

Cam decided to skip his last year of college and go to the NFL. The NFL gets to pick the best college players each year in what's called a **draft**. The Carolina Panthers got the first choice in the 2011 draft. They chose Cam. The Panthers hoped Cam could be the quarterback to lead them to the Super Bowl.

The Panthers play in Charlotte, North Carolina. They weren't playing very well before they got Cam. They won only two games in 2010. They hoped Cam would make them a lot better. The Panthers agreed to pay Cam $22 million dollars over four years. That's a lot of money! But they thought Cam would be worth it.

The Carolina Panthers chose Cam as their number one
pick during the NFL draft. Cam wears #1 on his jersey.

A FAST START

Cam got off to a great start with the Panthers. He threw the ball for 422 yards in his first game. That set a record! That was more yards than any rookie quarterback had ever thrown in one game. The team lost that first game. But Cam showed the fans how good he was. In his second game, Cam broke his own record. He passed for 432 yards against the Green Bay Packers.

Cam kept on breaking records. Against the Tampa Bay Buccaneers, Cam ran the ball for his 13th touchdown. That broke the record for most rushing touchdowns by an NFL quarterback. Later on, Cam became the first NFL quarterback to throw for 4,000 yards and run for 500 yards in a single season.

Cam tries to avoid a tackle by the Atlanta Falcons. Cam is a much better runner than most NFL quarterbacks.

SUPERMAN TO THE RESCUE

A quarterback is the leader of the football team. Cam has the **qualities** of a leader. He works really hard, and he's very **competitive**. "I want to be the best," Cam said during his first season at Carolina. "I want to be the **symbol** of success in this league."

Cam is very serious about winning. But he also smiles and jokes around a lot. He likes to have fun. Sometimes after a touchdown Cam will pretend to rip off his shirt like Superman. That has become one of his celebration **poses**. Do you think Cam really has super powers? He sure plays like it!

Cam celebrates after scoring a touchdown against the Chicago Bears. He pretends to tear off his shirt like Superman.

RECORD BREAKER

In Cam's first season, the Panthers lost some close games. The team's record was 6-10. The team didn't have a great year. But Cam had a great year. He had one of the best rookie seasons ever. He broke lots of records. His biggest **accomplishment** may be that he threw for 4,051 yards. That broke Peyton Manning's record for most passing yards by an NFL rookie quarterback.

With Cam's talent, he will probably break a lot more records in the future. Will Cam ever win the Super Bowl? He has the talent to win a lot of Super Bowls. He has the talent to be one of the greatest quarterbacks of all time. Cam Newton is one of football's fastest rising stars!

Cam escapes a tackle by the Tampa Bay Buccaneers. Cam can avoid lots of tackles. He's really fast and strong.

RECORD BOOK

CAM NEWTON
2010 HEISMAN TROPHY WINNER
AUBURN UNIVERSITY
QUARTERBACK

	Passing Stats	Rushing Stats
	Yards/Touchdowns	Yards/Touchdowns
Year Team		
2010 AUBURN	2,854 yds./30 TDs	1,473 yds./20 TDs

SINGLE SEASON COLLEGE RECORDS

Most rushing yards by a Southeastern Conference (SEC) college quarterback— 1,473

First SEC quarterback to throw for 2,000 yards and run for 1,000 yards

Most total yards of offense by an SEC player—4,327

CAM NEWTON
BIRTH DATE: 5-11-89
BIRTHPLACE: SAVANNAH, GEORGIA
HEIGHT: 6' 5"   WEIGHT: 250 LBS.

	Passing Stats	Rushing Stats
	Yards/Touchdowns	Yards/Touchdowns
Year Team		
2011 PANTHERS	4,051 yds./21 TDs	706 yds./14 TDs

NFL SINGLE SEASON RECORDS

Most passing yards by an NFL rookie quarterback—4,051

Most rushing touchdowns by an NFL quarterback—14

First NFL player to throw for 4,000 yards and run for 500 yards

GLOSSARY

ACCOMPLISHMENT (uh-KOM-plish-munt) Something to be proud of; something you've done a good job with.

BACK-UP (BAK-up) To be the second choice for something.

COMPETITIVE (kum-PET-uh-tiv) To try really hard to win.

DRAFT (Draft) A time when the NFL chooses new players for the teams.

JUNIOR COLLEGE (JUNE-yur KA-lij) A two-year school that people can attend after high school.

OPPONENTS (uh-PO-nunts) Teams you play against.

POSE (Poze) To put your body in a certain position; to pretend to be someone else.

QUALITIES (KWAL-uh-tees) Features that make people who they are.

ROOKIE (RUK-e) A first-year player in a sports league.

RUSHING (RUSH-ing) Running the football.

SYMBOL (SIM-bul) Something that stands for something. Something that represents.

TALENT (TAL-unt) An ability to be really good at something.

TRANSFER (TRANS-fur) To move to another school.

INDEX

WEB SITES

Due to the changing nature of Internet links, PowerKids Press has developed an online list of Web sites related to the subject of this book. This site is updated regularly. Please use this link to access the list:
www.powerkidslinks.com/frs/newton/